T0002526

What is a Sea Dog?

Why it's any dog who loves the water,
Or lives along the shore.

Skunk kept things fun on the *Eastwind* in 1947. Skunk's thick coat came in handy on cold missions to Greenland. The ship was one of the United States Coast Guard's first true icebreakers.

Whose tail wags and ears jump
When stormy winds roar.

It's any dog who dreams of fish
While drinking water from her dish.

Some dogs eat fish. Portuguese Water Dogs herd them. For hundreds of years they helped fishermen catch fish. Their diving skills inspired Joan Lehman's painting.

A swimming dog with big webbed feet,
Diving with his hair so neat.

Portuguese Water Dog Ace's fancy hairstyle keeps him warm and quick in the water. Webbed feet and a rudder-like tail make him a great swimmer.

Giant dogs who fight the surf,

Nathan held his breath. Then the dog's head bobbed to the surface. The boy tossed the bow line to Sirius. The dog caught it in his teeth and paddled in place, waiting.

Strong and furry, Newfoundland dogs can pull ropes, boats, and people through cold rough water. A real rescue on the Maine Coast inspired the book *Sirius the Dog Star*, written by Angeli Perrow and illustrated by Emily Harris.

Saving swimmers on their turf.

Over his long life, Bob saved 23 people from England's River Thames. The stray Newfoundland inspired a famous 19th-century dog painting. Look for copies in surprising places, like this hand-painted teacup.

A dog who
guards the
Captain's back,
With eyes so
bold and hair
so black.

In 1859, the magnificent
Newfoundland Wallace
helped Captain Samuel
Samuels put down a
mutiny. Wallace kept
lookout and pinned one
mutineer to the deck
with his big paws. The
clipper ship made it
safely to New York.

8

A little quick dog small and fierce!
Chasing boys with teeth that pierce!

The big *Peking* faced many Cape Horn storms. In 1929, sea dog Mauritz kept a crew of young cadets safe and in good form. A quick nip from his sharp German teeth made the sailor boys move fast during shipboard drills.

Dogs that face the dangers deep

Submarines sank many ships during World War II. This little mascot dog, "The Last Man Off" was lucky. Coast Guard rescuers carried him to safety.

Dogs who face them fast asleep.

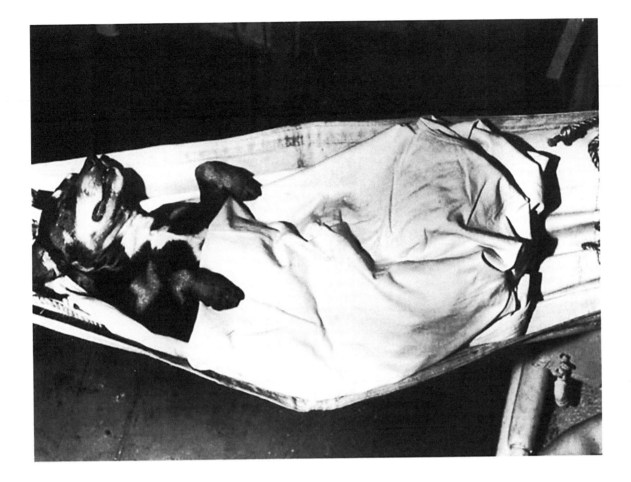

Submarine dangers are no worry for salty Sinbad. He snoozes in his hammock on the Coast Guard cutter *Campbell*.

Courageous dogs who cross the sea
Bringing cheer and victory.

On duty Sinbad, Dog First Class, looks for enemy submarines. He is helping protect Allied cargo ships that are slowly crossing the Atlantic Ocean.

Coast Guard dogs, thousands strong
Patrolling beaches all night long.

In 1942, America needed to protect her coast from foreign agents. Two thousand sea dogs joined the new Coast Guard Beach Patrol. This sea dog and his human walked a lonely Oregon beach.

Dogs on ice who look for whales,

Northern peoples used dogs to cross the frozen seas. Whaling Captain and photographer George Comer learned about Arctic life in Hudson Bay from his native friends and their icy sea dogs.

Dogs on ships with snapping sails.

Sea dogs rarely complain and they make fine shipmates. This pup sailed from New York to London on the tiny ship *Red, White, and Blue* in 1866.

Dogs that bark out orders: Avast!

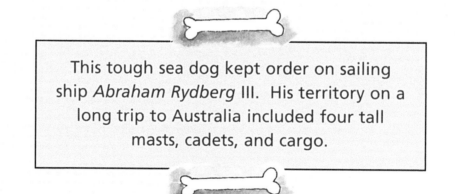

This tough sea dog kept order on sailing ship *Abraham Rydberg* III. His territory on a long trip to Australia included four tall masts, cadets, and cargo.

But giving love down to the last.

Rough hands felt smooth on this little sea dog. He served on an ocean science ship around 1910.

Of all these dogs across the sea,

Hundreds of dogs lifted spirits on ships during World War II. Blackout, an ancestor of our little Skipper, served on a landing craft operated by Coast Guardsmen. He hit the beaches at the invasions of Sicily, Italy, and Normandy.

What kind of sea dog Do YOU want to be?

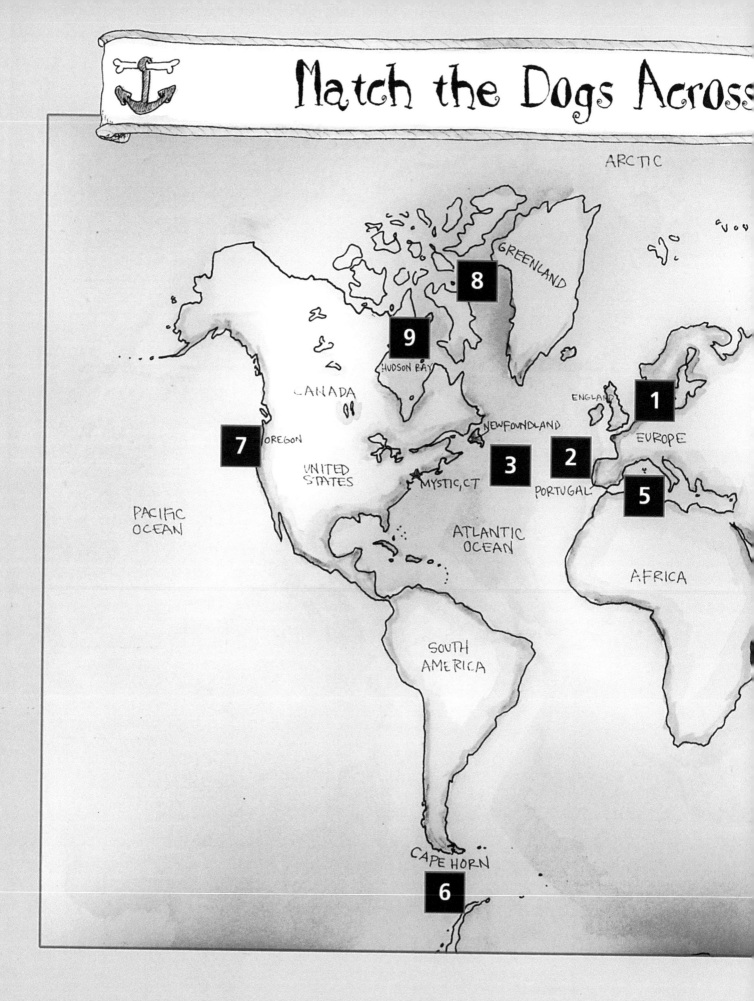

the Sea

ASIA

PACIFIC OCEAN

INDIAN OCEAN

AUSTRALIA

4

Find & Match

Match the Sea Dog pictures with the numbers on the Map to show where each Sea Dog traveled. (Look at each dog's page for clues. The answers are on the last page.)

A. _____

B. _____

C. _____

D. _____

E. _____

F. _____

G. _____

H. _____

I. _____

Mystic Seaport

Credits

Pages 2-3: Courtesy of the United States Coast Guard Historian's Office, Washington, DC.

Page 4: Courtesy of the artist, Joan Lehman, and Terry Cardillino, editor of *The Currier*, The Official Publication of the Portuguese Water Dog Club of America.

Page 5: Kalista's Amazing Ace, courtesy of Alissa Behn, Pet Personalities-Photography by Alissa, and *The Currier*, The Official Publication of the Portuguese Water Dog Club of America.

Page 6: From *Sirius, The Dog Star*, by Angeli Perrow, illustrated by Emily Harris (Camden, Maine: Down East Books, 2002), courtesy of Down East Books.

Page 7: China cup, ca. 1880, decorated with a miniature of Sir Edwin Landseer's 1838 painting *A Distinguished Member of the Humane Society*, courtesy of Janice Hight, Judy Beisler photo.

Page 8: Ogden's Cigarettes advertising card, Sea Adventure Series number 32, "The Mutiny of the Dreadnought," courtesy of Janice Hight.

Page 9: Photograph by Irving Johnson, 1929, courtesy of the National Maritime Historical Society, Peekskill, New York.

Page 10: Photograph by Lieutenant Commander Jack Dixon, Records of the United States Coast Guard, 1785-1988, Record Group 26, National Archives at College Park, College Park, MD.

Page 11: Records of the United States Coast Guard, 1785-1988, Record Group 26, National Archives at College Park, College Park, MD.

Page 12: Records of the United States Coast Guard, 1785-1988, Record Group 26, National Archives at College Park, College Park, MD.

Page 13: Courtesy of the United States Coast Guard Historian's Office, Washington, DC.

Page 14: Photograph by George Comer, ca. 1905, Mystic Seaport, 1966.339.21.

Page 15: Lithograph by Currier and Ives, ca. 1866, Mystic Seaport, 1939.1606.

Page 16: Photograph ca. 1940, Mystic Seaport, 1977.29.163.

Page 17: Photograph ca. 1910, Mystic Seaport, 1952.152.

Page 18 and Front Cover: Records of the United States Coast Guard, 1785-1988, Record Group 26, National Archives at College Park, College Park, MD.

Special thanks to Linda Cusano, Arleen Andersen, and Karen Belmore.

Answers to Match the Dogs Across the Sea
A: 2; B: 1; C: 8; D: 7; E: 6; F: 3; G: 4; H: 9; I: 5

Published by Muddy Boots/Mystic Seaport Museum
An imprint of Globe Pequot, the trade division of
The Rowman & Littlefield Publishing Group, Inc.
4501 Forbes Blvd., Ste. 200
Lanham, MD 20706
www.rowman.com

MuddyBootsBooks.com

Distributed by NATIONAL BOOK NETWORK

Copyright © 2003 by Mystic Seaport Museum, Inc.
First Muddy Boots edition 2023

Reprinted by the Rowman & Littlefield Publishing Group in 2023

All rights reserved. No part of this book may be reproduced in any form or by any electronic or mechanical means, including information storage and retrieval systems, without written permission from the publisher, except by a reviewer who may quote passages in a review.

British Library Cataloguing in Publication Information available

Library of Congress Cataloging-in-Publication Data Available
ISBN 9781493073269 (pbk. : alk. paper)
ISBN 9781493076529 (e-book)

♾™ The paper used in this publication meets the minimum requirements of American National Standard for Information Sciences—Permanence of Paper for Printed Library Materials, ANSI/NISO Z39.48-1992.